Ten Po about Roses

ex libris

Candlestick Press

C000003501

Published by:

Candlestick Press,
Diversity House, 72 Nottingham Road, Arnold, Nottingham NG5 6LF
www.candlestickpress.co.uk

Design and typesetting by Craig Twigg

Printed by Ratcliff & Roper Print Group, Nottinghamshire, UK

Selection © Katharine Towers, 2022

Cover illustration © Jane Walker, 2022
https://www.janewalkerprintmaker.com

Candlestick Press monogram © Barbara Shaw, 2008

© Candlestick Press, 2022

ISBN 978 1 913627 05 8

Acknowledgements

The poems in this pamphlet are reprinted from the following books, all by
permission of the publishers listed unless stated otherwise. Every effort has been
made to trace the copyright holders of the poems published in this book. The
editor and publisher apologise if any material has been included without
permission or without the appropriate acknowledgement, and would be glad to be
told of anyone who has not been consulted.

Thanks are due to all the copyright holders cited below for their kind permission:

Alistair Te Ariki Campbell, *The Collected Poems of Alistair Te Ariki Campbell*,
(Victoria University of Wellington Press, 2016) by kind permission of the Estate
of Alistair Te Ariki Campbell. David Constantine, *Collected Poems* (Bloodaxe
Books, 2006) www.bloodaxebooks.com. Stanley Plumly, *Middle Distance:
Poems* (WW Norton & Co., 2020). Eloise Unerman, *Wild Poetry* (Hive, 2017) by
kind permission of the poet. Jean Valentine, *Little Boat* (Wesleyan Poetry, 2007).

All permissions cleared courtesy of Suzanne Fairless-Aitken
c/o Swift Permissions swiftpermissions@gmail.com

Where poets are no longer living, their dates are given.

Contents

Ophelia Roses

Out of the dawn
Trembling with moon-mist
The glow of a sun-gold rose!
Wild as a wood-bird note,
Fragrant as crushed red wine.

Lucy Eddy (1863 – 1931)

Rosa Canina
(Common name: Dog Rose)

Her spine was curved from climbing, her half-covered
red hips, the first whisper of another autumn.

She bears freckles along smile lines, somehow
found in days weaving away from insects

and blackbirds, trying to get off the ground,
rubbing dirt from her knees and singing

for her family with a voice made of syrup.
When she finishes her tune, they'll carve

out the part of her that itches for something
more than sweet charm and climbing walls.

Eloise Unerman

The Rose

a labyrinth,
as if at its center,
god would be there –
but at the center, only rose,
where rose came from,
where rose grows –
& us, inside of the lips & lips:
the likenesses, the eyes, & the hair,
we are born of,
fed by, & marry with,
only flesh itself, only its passage
– out of where?   to where?

Then god the mother said to Jim, in a dream,
Never mind you, Jim,
come rest again on the country porch of my knees.

Jean Valentine (1934 – 2020)

Kunitz Tending Roses

Naturally he doesn't hear too well,
so that when he's kneeling he's really
listening at the very mouth of the flower.
And the feeling in his hands, his sense
of touch, seems gloved if not quite gone,
though when he bleeds he takes a certain
notice, wipes it away, then moves on.

And winter eyes. The old have passion's
winter eyes, which see with a pointillist
chill clarity, but must look close, as his do,
petal by petal, since the work is tactile
visual: Cadenza, Blaze, Red Fountain climbing
or like free-standing rhododendron,
sunset gold Medallion, scarlet Maiden.

His body bends depending on the height
and cluster or, on a perfect scale, the stature
of the rose, which, like the day, declines
continually: meaning that toward evening
he almost disappears among the fragrance,
gala, and double flesh of roses: or when
he's upright, back to the sun, is thin

enough to see through, thorn and bone.
Still, there he is, on any given day,
talking to ramblers, floribundas, Victorian
perpetuals, as if for beauty and to make us
glad or otherwise for envy and to make us
wish for more – if only to mystify and move us.
The damasked, dusky hundred-petaled heart.

Interrogate the rose, ask the old,
who have the seminal patience of flowers,
which question nothing, less for why we ask:
Enchanter, Ember, Blood Talisman, something
to summarize the color of desire, aureate
or red passion, something on fire to hold
in the hand, the hand torn with caring.

Stanley Plumly (1939 – 2019)

Ashes and Roses

She is size 10 again like the girl under her banns
But so disconsolate the falling of her hand
I worry the diamond will slip to the grey earth.

These are only the bare bones of roses
This is a garden of little twists of iron
The dressing of ash does not look nourishing.

Let me look away at the sunny hills and you
Look at nothing for a while against my heart.
You feel as breakable as things I have found on the hills

After the weather when their small frames are evident.
You need to put on again
The roses need to flower. Come home

To your empty house. He is more there than here

David Constantine

The Rose

The lily has a smooth stalk,
  Will never hurt your hand;
But the rose upon her briar
  Is lady of the land.

There's sweetness in an apple tree,
  And profit in the corn;
But lady of all beauty
  Is a rose upon a thorn.

When with moss and honey
  She tips her bending briar,
And half unfolds her glowing heart,
  She sets the world on fire.

Christina Rossetti (1830 – 1894)

Rose of all the World

I am here myself; as though this heave of effort
At starting other life, fulfilled my own:
Rose-leaves that whirl in colour round a core
Of seed-specks kindled lately and softly blown

By all the blood of the rose-bush into being –
Strange, that the urgent will in me, to set
My mouth on hers in kisses, and so softly
To bring together two strange sparks, beget

Another life from our lives, so should send
The innermost fire of my own dim soul out-spinning
And whirling in blossom of flame and being upon me!
That my completion of manhood should be the beginning

Another life from mine! For so it looks.
The seed is purpose, blossom accident.
The seed is all in all, the blossom lent
To crown the triumph of this new descent.

Is that it, woman? Does it strike you so?
The Great Breath blowing a tiny seed of fire
Fans out your petals for excess of flame,
Till all your being smokes with fine desire?

Or are we kindled, you and I, to be
One rose of wonderment upon the tree
Of perfect life, and is our possible seed
But the residuum of the ecstasy?

How will you have it? – the rose is all in all,
Or the ripe rose-fruits of the luscious fall?
The sharp begetting, or the child begot?
Our consummation matters, or does it not?

To me it seems the seed is just left over
From the red-rose flowers' fiery transience;
Just orts and slarts; berries that smoulder in the bush
Which burnt just now with marvellous immanence.

Blossom, my darling, blossom, be a rose
Of roses unchidden and purposeless; a rose
For rosiness only, without an ulterior motive;
For me it is more than enough if the flower unclose.

DH Lawrence (1885 – 1930)

Words and Roses

I never imagined so rare a night
would make me dream of roses –
the gentle rain,
the words falling irresistibly
as arrows in flight,
sometimes singly,
sometimes in a shower,
far too many for me to catch,
and each a flower
without match.
In what other life did you wear them
so that they smelt of you?
We knew each other well,
these words and I,
from having sung of you everywhere
under your spell.
I followed them to the source
somewhere north of your heart –
or was it more to the south?
It matters only that they came,
from whichever direction,
still warm from your mouth.
Dear heart, I had forgotten everything
I learnt that love disposes,
until last night they came again
in a dream
with the gentle rain,
smelling of you and roses.

– Christmas Day, 1998

Alistair Te Ariki Campbell (1925 – 2009)

The Rose

Beneath my chamber window
Pierrot was singing, singing;
   I heard his lute the whole night thru
      Until the east was red.
Alas, alas Pierrot,
I had no rose for flinging
   Save one that drank my tears for dew
      Before its leaves were dead.

I found it in the darkness,
I kissed it once and threw it,
   The petals scattered over him,
      His song was turned to joy;
And he will never know –
Alas, the one who knew it! –
   The rose was plucked when dusk was dim
      Beside a laughing boy.

Sara Teasdale (1884 – 1933)

A sepal – petal – and a thorn

A sepal – petal – and a thorn
Upon a common summer's morn –
A flask of Dew – A Bee or two –
A Breeze – a caper in the trees –
    And I'm a Rose!

Emily Dickinson (1830 – 1886)